MINMI
and Other Dinosaurs of Australia
by Dougal Dixon

illustrated by
Steve Weston and James Field

PICTURE WINDOW BOOKS
Minneapolis, Minnesota

Picture Window Books
5115 Excelsior Boulevard
Suite 232
Minneapolis, MN 55416
877-845-8392
www.picturewindowbooks.com

Printed in the United States of America.

Library of Congress Cataloging-in-Publication Data
Dixon, Dougal.
Minmi and other dinosaurs of Australia / by Dougal
Dixon ; illustrated by Steve Weston & James Field.
p. cm. — (Dinosaur find)
Includes bibliographical references and index.
ISBN-13: 978-1-4048-2262-7 (library binding)
ISBN-10: 1-4048-2262-3 (library binding)
ISBN-13: 978-1-4048-2268-9 (paperback)
ISBN-10: 1-4048-2268-2 (paperback)
1. Dinosaurs–Australia–Juvenile literature.
I. Weston, Steve, ill. II. Field, James, 1959- ill. III. Title.
QE861.5.D62 2007
567.90994—dc22   2006027943

Acknowledgments
This book was produced for Picture Window Books by
Bender Richardson White, U.K.

Illustrations by James Field (pages 4–5, 7, 13, 15, 19)
and Steve Weston (cover and pages 9, 11, 17, 21).
Diagrams by Stefan Chabluk.

Photographs: Corbis page 16. istockphotos pages 6
(Gordon Laurens), 8 (jason crabb), 10 (Steffen
Foerster), 12 (Neil Wigmore), 14 (Ron Kacmarcik), 18
(Norman Reid), 20 (Holly Kuchera).

Consultant: John Stidworthy, Scientific Fellow of
the Zoological Society, London, and former
Lecturer in the Education Department, Natural History
Museum, London.

Reading Adviser: Susan Kesselring, M.A., Literacy
Educator, Rosemount–Apple Valley–Eagan
(Minnesota) School District

Types of dinosaurs
In this book, a red shape at the
top of a left-hand page shows
the animal was a meat-eater.
A green shape shows it was
a plant-eater.

**Just how big—or small—
were they?**
Dinosaurs were many different
sizes. We have compared their
size to one of the following:

Chicken
2 feet (60 centimeters) tall
Weight 6 pounds (2.7 kilograms)

Adult person
6 feet (1.8 meters) tall
Weight 170 pounds (76.5 kg)

Elephant
10 feet (3 m) tall
Weight 12,000 pounds
(5,400 kg)

TABLE OF CONTENTS

WHAT'S INSIDE?

Dinosaurs! These dinosaurs lived in the land now called Australia. Find out how they survived millions of years ago and what they have in common with today's animals.

LIFE IN AUSTRALIA

Dinosaurs lived between 230 million and 65 million years ago. The world did not look the same then. Much of the land and many of the seas were not in the same places as today. But even then, the land of Australia formed a continent of its own. And it had a unique collection of animals, including dinosaurs.

On the edge of a forest, a herd of small and swift-footed *Leaellynasaura* was chased by a hunting *Timimus*. A big plant-eater, *Muttaburrasaurus*, looked on.

5

LEAELLYNASAURA

Pronunciation:
lay-EL-in-ah-SAW-rah

People often think of dinosaurs living only in the warm climates of deserts and jungles. However, *Leaellynasaura* put up with cold weather and snow. Long ago, the climate of southern Australia was quite cold.

Cold climates today

Modern grouse live in snow-covered landscapes, like *Leaellynasaura* did 115 million years ago.

Size Comparison

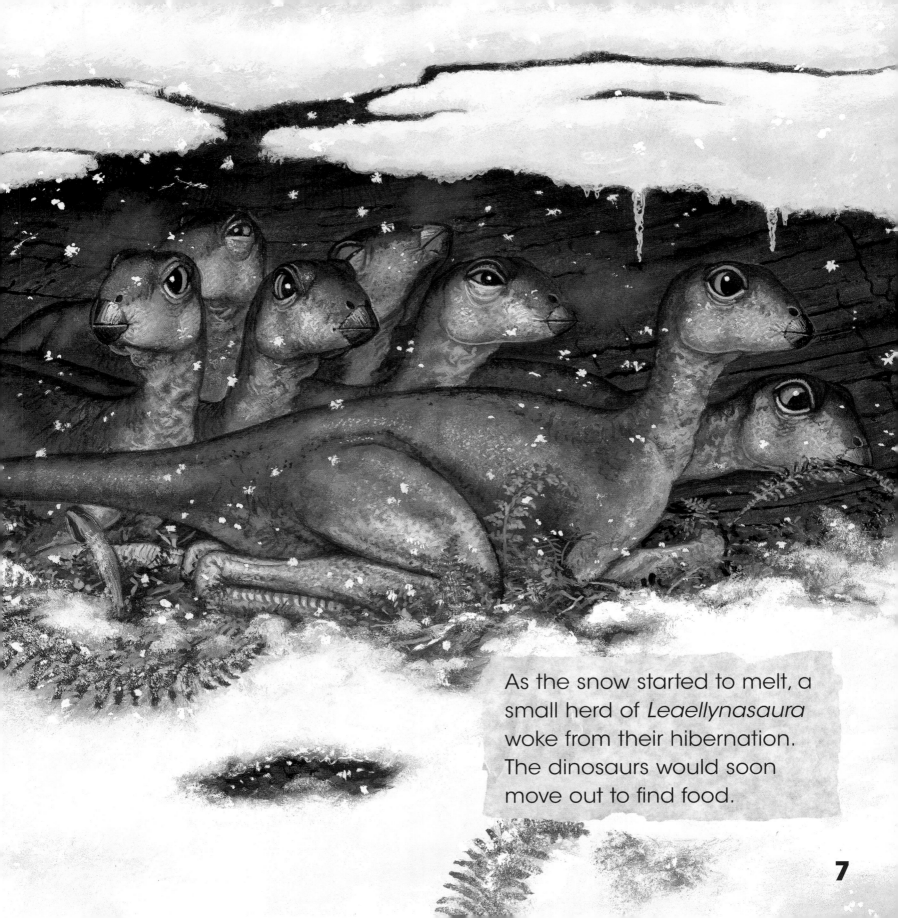

As the snow started to melt, a small herd of *Leaellynasaura* woke from their hibernation. The dinosaurs would soon move out to find food.

MINMI

Pronunciation:
MIN-mee

Minmi was an armored dinosaur found only in ancient Australia. Its back and belly were covered in tough plates. *Minmi* also had spikes over its hips and tail. It may have used the spikes for protection and as weapons.

Spiky Australian today

The echidna, or spiny anteater, has spines on its back. Like the armor of *Minmi*, the spines protect it from enemies.

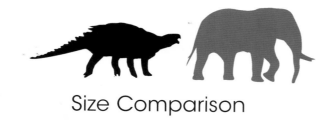

Size Comparison

A *Minmi* turned to face two meat-eating *Ozraptor*. The *Minmi* raised its armored tail, ready to swing if an attacker came near.

ATLASCOPCOSAURUS

Pronunciation:
AT-lus-KOP-ko-SAW-rus

Atlascopcosaurus ate small plants such as ferns. It used its sharp beak to nip the best buds and leaves. *Atlascopcosaurus* had a long tail and long legs, which helped it outrun dinosaurs on the hunt for a good meal.

Forest runner today

The modern okapi feeds on short plants, has a long tail, and uses its long legs to escape enemies, just as *Atlascopcosaurus* did long ago.

Size Comparison

Atlascopcosaurus sometimes climbed rocky hills to find plants to eat. In a landslide, it spread its arms, legs, and tail to avoid falling.

11

TIMIMUS

Pronunciation:
tee-MYE-mus

Timimus was a lightweight hunting dinosaur. Using long, powerful hind legs, it chased after plant-eating dinosaurs. Then *Timimus* used sharp claws to tear apart the prey before eating it. *Timimus* also ran away from larger meat-eaters on the hunt.

Fast animals today

Springbok are light animals that live in open country and use speed to escape their enemies, much like *Timimus* did.

Size Comparison

Moving in open country, *Timimus* was always looking for prey to chase and eat. It also kept a lookout for any dinosaurs that would eat a *Timimus*.

13

AUSTROSAURUS

Pronunciation:
OSS-tro-SAW-rus

Many long-necked, plant-eating dinosaurs lived in ancient Australia. *Austrosaurus* was one of them. It lived along seashores, eating from trees that grew there. *Austrosaurus* died on seashores, too. Its remains gradually turned into fossils.

Seashore animals today

Today, scavengers such as seagulls fly along seashores looking for the remains of dead animals. In the time of *Austrosaurus*, the *Pterosaurs* did the same.

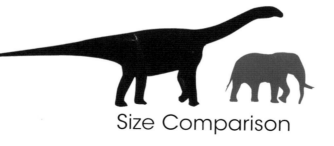

Size Comparison

14

Two flying reptiles called *Pterosaurs* circled near an *Austrosaurus*. They were looking for scraps of food. They would eat the remains of dead *Austrosaurus* and other animals.

15

OZRAPTOR

Pronunciation:
oz-RAP-tur

Ozraptor was one of the fiercest hunters among ancient Australia's dinosaurs. *Ozraptor* had powerful jaws with sharp teeth, and big, sharp claws on its hands and feet. It mostly hunted large plant-eating dinosaurs.

Scavengers today

Modern vultures like to eat meat. They feed on animals killed by other predators, as *Ozraptor* sometimes did.

Size Comparison

Ozraptor was a scavenger as well as a hunter. Following a forest fire, *Ozraptor* would eat the remains of dead animals.

17

Muttaburrasaurus was a big dinosaur that ate plants. It moved mostly on all fours but could also walk on just its hind legs. *Muttaburrasaurus* could use its hands to pull down branches to eat. This dinosaur had a broad, duck-like beak and a big bump on its nose.

Treetop feeders today

Modern giraffes feed on leaves at the tops of trees, just as *Muttaburrasaurus* did.

Size Comparison

To eat, *Muttaburrasaurus* could grab limbs or stretch out its neck and tear leaves from branches with its beak.

19

RHOETOSAURUS

Pronunciation:
ROH-tuh-SAW-rus

Rhoetosaurus was the biggest dinosaur in the region. It grew to 40 feet (11.5 meters) in length. *Rhoetosaurus* was a long-necked plant-eater with a big tail. It probably lived in herds to protect against large meat-eaters.

Herds today

Wild horses live in herds as *Rhoetosaurus* probably did. They stay together when running from a predator. That way, the predator does not know which horse to chase.

Size Comparison

While looking for food along the edges of forests, *Rhoetosaurus* had to be fearful of large predators hunting there.

WHERE DID THEY GO?

Dinosaurs are extinct, which means that none of them are alive today. Scientists study rocks and fossils to find clues about what happened to dinosaurs.

People have different explanations about what happened. Some people think a huge asteroid hit Earth and caused all sorts of climate changes, which caused the dinosaurs to die. Others think volcanic eruptions caused the climate to change and that killed the dinosaurs. No one knows for sure what happened to all of the dinosaurs.

GLOSSARY

armor—protective covering of plates, horns, spikes, or clubs used for fighting

beak—the hard front part of the mouth of birds and some dinosaurs; also called a bill

claws—tough, usually curved fingernails or toenails

continent—a huge area of land like North America or Asia

ferns—plants with finely divided leaves known as fronds; ferns are common in damp woods and along rivers

fossils—the remains of a plant or animal that lived between thousands and millions of years ago

hibernation—a long winter sleep of some animals in cold climates; the animals may wake from time to time to eat

plate—a large, flat, usually tough structure on the body

prey—animals that are hunted by other animals for food; the hunters are known as predators

scavenger—a meat-eater that feeds on animals that are already dead

To Learn More

At the Library

Clark, Neil, and William Lindsay. *1001 Facts About Dinosaurs*. New York: Backpack Books, Dorling Kindersley, 2002.

Dixon, Dougal. *Dougal Dixon's Amazing Dinosaurs*. Honesdale, Pa.: Boyds Mills Press, 2000.

Holtz, Thomas, and Michael Brett-Surman. *Dinosaur Field Guide*. New York: Random House, 2001.

On the Web

FactHound offers a safe, fun way to find Web sites related to this book. All of the sites on FactHound have been researched by our staff.

1. Visit *www.facthound.com*
2. Type in this special code: 1404822623
3. Click on the FETCH IT button.

Your trusty FactHound will fetch the best Web sites for you!

Index

Look for all of the books in the Dinosaur Find series: